S THE
SUPERVISOR'S
GUIDE

S THE UPERVISOR'S GUIDE

Jerry Brown
and
Denise Dudley

SkillPath Publications
Mission, Kansas

Library of Congress Catalog Card Number: 95-71728

ISBN: 1-878-542-01-X

10   9   8   7   6   5   4   3   2   1   01   02   03   04   05

Printed in the United States of America

CONTENTS

PREFACE

Supervising others can be as rewarding as it is challenging if you approach the job with intelligence, creativity, a good sense of humor, and a basic knowledge of what it takes to work with and motivate others.

As a supervisor, you don't have to learn everything by doing. You can give yourself the edge by learning ideas and techniques that have proven valuable for other supervisors and managers. In this book, we share with you those secrets to success — and help you build on your own experience.

This guide will be a useful aid in approaching your challenges as a supervisor. Of course, the suggestions we offer are just that — suggestions. They are not intended to replace your organization's policies or to override your own experience and beliefs. Rather, our intent is to help you shape your own good judgment for deciding on the course of action to take in any situation.

We wish you the best as a manager or supervisor — persevere through the challenges and, more important, celebrate the successes!

Sincerely,
Jerry Brown
Denise Dudley

HOW TO CHOOSE A SUPERVISORY STYLE

Ask yourself these questions: Who was the best supervisor I ever worked for? What did that person do?

When a group of people share their answers to the second question, an interesting variety of answers are provided.

Some people say:
> "He gave us clear instructions about what we should do."
> "She was well organized; procedures were carefully defined."
> "We were rewarded fairly for what we did."
> "He knew the job well and set an excellent example."
> "She was businesslike and thorough."

The people who offered those responses are describing what might be called a *task-centered* supervisor.

Other people say:
> "She always was willing to discuss our suggestions and complaints."
> "He was patient and understanding when we were learning new things."
> "We trusted her, and she trusted us."
> "You could always count on him caring about you as a person."
> "She was warm and good-humored."

These responses describe a *people-centered* supervisor.

If your company were hiring a new manager to supervise your work and you could choose one type of person or the other, which would you prefer?

Some people would pick the task-centered person, some would pick the people-centered person, and some would want a combination.

Why? The reason might lie in the person or in the work situation.

Some people are themselves one kind of person or the other, and people generally prefer working closely with someone similar to themselves. They know people are more likely to understand and approve of others who are like them, so they feel more comfortable with someone similar than with someone different.

Some work situations call more for one kind of supervisor than for the other. The organizational culture in some companies favors a particular kind of supervisory style. For example, many technically oriented firms, such as manufacturing or data-processing companies, think and talk in terms of what it takes to get a job done correctly—task issues. Many service organizations, such as health care providers or advertising agencies, think and talk about the impact their activities have on how individuals feel—people issues.

Workers also influence what style is preferred. For example, well-trained, intelligent, highly motivated employees know how to do their jobs well and need a minimum of task-oriented leadership from their supervisors. Beginners, who are insecure about performing their jobs, need a lot of task direction. When there's ample time to get a job done and it requires creative thought, a people-centered style is more suitable.

Table 1 provides guidelines for choosing a supervisory style.

Table 1   **Appropriate Supervisory Styles**

Work Situation	Supervisory Style
1. People are confused or upset, (e.g., there's a parts shortage or an equipment failure)	Task-centered
2. Complex technology, inexperienced employees	Task-centered
3. Undesirable, but simple and repetitive job	People-centered
4. Self-sufficient, capable workers performing complex job	People-centered
5. Emotionally immature workers, average skill level	Task-centered
6. Employees are "prima donnas," but very talented	People-centered
7. Employees are highly interdependent, so coordination by supervisor is essential	Task-centered; people-centeredness depends on emotional maturity of workers
8. Volunteers who could quit at any point	People-centered
9. Employees dislike work	Both task- and people-centered
10. Start-up of new operation, vague job descriptions	Both task- and people-centered
11. Inexperienced, but well-meaning employees	Both task- and people-centered

Clearly, there is no one best way to lead people. The competent supervisor is able to be both task- and people-centered when each is appropriate. The trick is knowing when to be each. The best supervisors are not robots acting out a precise script. They diagnose the people and situation they are in and then choose a course of action likely to achieve good results.

HOW TO COMMUNICATE EFFECTIVELY

THE IMPORTANCE OF EFFECTIVE COMMUNICATION

Supervisors spend about 75 percent of their work time communicating. How they handle communication affects their performance—better communication yields better results, both for the company and their own careers.

Communication is a critical factor in success—it distinguishes those who succeed from those who don't—because it is much more difficult than it seems. Most people believe they communicate very well. Yet they also believe most other people communicate poorly. In other words, we tend to exaggerate our own ability to communicate.

Why? Because we picture what we are saying when we speak and assume our words evoke the same picture in our listeners' minds. That's not necessarily so—or even likely. So it is common to presume that we are getting our message across when actually we are being completely misunderstood.

Also, as listeners, we tend to assume we understand what others are saying. Actually, we may be greatly misinterpreting their intentions.

Why these misunderstandings? Many possible reasons exist. Chief among them is how differently people expect others to behave. Suppose your boss thinks that people who really care about their organizations do most of the important jobs themselves. However, you might think that people who care about their organizations delegate important jobs to others, so they will have a chance to grow. One day, your boss inquires about an important favor she recently asked of you. You tell her you delegated the task to one of your best employees. She expected you to do the task yourself. She assumes that you do not care about her or the work—so she feels hurt and angry. Actually, you meant to convey that you value it highly. A miscommunication has occurred. It could cost you that relationship — unless you can overcome the communication barriers.

OVERCOMING COMMUNICATION BARRIERS

Watch out for inadequate listening. People often use the time they should spend listening to think about how they will reply. As a result, they miss important parts of the message or misinterpret the speaker's intent. Before ending a conversation, it is a good idea to summarize what a person has said to you. Or, ask the person you're speaking with questions such as, "Okay, what have we agreed upon?" or "Basically, what have you heard me saying?"

Appeal to the interests of the receiver. People listen most attentively to messages that promise to satisfy a need. For example, if you want volunteers to do a relatively unpleasant task, you could present the task straightforwardly and wait for a response. Or, you could introduce your request by asking, "Who would like to be a real hero around here?" or "I'm in real trouble here and I need someone's help," or "I've got a task here that will earn someone an extra bonus." By recognizing that people do things for their reasons, not yours, you will get ideas across much more effectively.

Confront preconceived ideas. If people start out disagreeing with you, they will not be receptive to your message. If you acknowledge their initial viewpoint, you stand a better chance of opening their minds to a new idea. If you want truck drivers to obey the 55-mile-per-hour speed limit, you might start out by saying, "I know you think that speed limits are for poor drivers, not you" or "I know you think it's costing you money to stick to the speed limit." By indicating that you understand how the situation looks to them, you lower their defenses to you and your argument, and make them more ready to listen.

Beware of differences in meaning. Many people think every word has a single, correct definition, and they expect everyone to interpret everything they say the same way. For example, a boss told an employee: "This job is important. Do it as soon as you have a chance." At the end of the day, the boss went to pick up the work. It had not been done, and he was very upset. The employee didn't understand why and he explained that he didn't have "a chance" that day to do the job and planned to do it tomorrow. He told the boss that if he wanted something done "right away," he should say so! The communication problem arose because the employee interpreted the instructions differently than his boss—a common occurrence.

Use bias-free language. A bias is a prejudgment of someone not based on fact. Biased attitudes often are reflected in the language people use to communicate. People assume a speaker is biased if he or she uses biased language such as "This work requires a real man" or "This is woman's work." Instead, the speaker could describe the qualities he or she seeks: "I need a persistent person" or "This work requires someone with good people skills." These statements do not close the door to anyone on the basis of gender alone. Obviously, demeaning jokes, derogatory names, or the use of any racist or sexist language, also indicate bias.

Repeat messages and avoid communication overload. People cannot assimilate everything they hear. Listeners remember only a fraction of what is said in most lectures or at most meetings and forget the rest. To be sure listeners remember the part of your messages you want them to recall:

- Clarify for yourself what is most important and be sure to repeat that core message several times, using slightly different wording each time to avoid boredom.
- Do not overload your audience with more information than it can use.

HOW TO MANAGE YOUR TIME

In today's increasingly complex and lean organizations, time is a supervisor's most precious possession. Almost everyone has many more things to do than time to do them in. Budgeting time and using it as efficiently as possible is essential for supervisors to be successful and to minimize stress. Follow these principles for using time effectively.

Value your time. Successful people recognize that their time is valuable. Divide your weekly salary by the number of hours you work and then divide that figure by 60 to determine how much every minute of your time is worth. You'll soon realize that idle chatter at the water cooler, a lengthy phone call, a two-hour lunch break or a purposeless meeting can be surprisingly expensive.

Value neatness and orderliness. An orderly desk, file cabinet and work area do not necessarily reflect an orderly mind, but they do help people be more productive and time-efficient. The less time you spend hunting for information when you need it, the more time you have for doing important work.

Value punctuality. When you and people who work for you are on time for appointments and meetings, much wasted time is eliminated. Of course, people behind in their work often hate to break away from it to be where they are expected. Yet making the effort to be prompt frees time for everyone to get more work done in the long run. Being punctual also helps you establish credibility—people who realize that you mean

---

THE SUPERVISOR'S GUIDE 9

and do what you say are more likely to do what you want when you ask. Being punctual also lowers your stress level—you feel less upset about being behind schedule.

Avoid perfectionism. Doing things right is important. But there also is a point of diminishing returns, when making more improvements simply delays completing a project and takes valuable time away from other endeavors. Stop periodically to take a "helicopter view." Step back from what you are doing, rise above the immediate situation, and consider the "big picture." Should you continue polishing what you are doing or let it go as is and move on to other things?

Appreciate the value of rest and recreation. It is true that most successful people work long hours, often 45-60 hours a week. But such people also realize that a good night's sleep, exercise and escape from the pressures of work allow them to recharge and return to work feeling more invigorated.

Prepare a "to-do" list and set priorities. At the end of every work day—or at the start of each new day—make a list of the things you want to accomplish the next day. Sort them into three categories:

> A = Most important (the highest payoff)
> B = Of some importance (keeps things going)
> C = Of little importance (can be delayed, delegated or eliminated)

Be sure to start the day with your highest priority "A" activities and then continue with "B" items before doing the least important things. Include on your list some future-oriented activities—such as asking about opportunities in your company's new division—so you don't spend your time just putting out fires.

Some people keep separate personal and work-related "to-do" lists; others combine them. Try both, then do what suits you.

Delegate whatever you can. The trend in supervision today is giving more responsibility, including decision-making authority, to the people actually doing the work. People generally respond well to having control over what they do. It gives them ownership and pride in their work. They prefer being given free rein to having someone looking over their shoulder with a critical eye. They usually will work especially hard to prove themselves worthy of that trust. Delegating work also preserves your time for doing more important things. Delegating assignments will be discussed in greater detail in another chapter.

Do not take on more than you can handle. Successful supervisors are judicious about the assignments they accept. They tactfully decline assignments when they are already fully scheduled.

How should you turn down an assignment from your boss? Very tactfully. Point out that it will interfere with carrying out other high-priority tasks. Then suggest alternatives, such as allowing you to hire temporary help or shifting some of your responsibilities to other departments to free up your time. Your boss will recognize that you are declining only because you want to do what is important, not to avoid work.

Don't procrastinate. Putting off unpleasant or intimidating tasks is a great waste of time. Having a great deal of "unfinished business" in your life also causes stress and distracts you from what you are doing at the time. To minimize procrastination:

- *Calculate the cost of delay.* Keep your mind on the rewards that will come when you complete the task and on what it will cost to delay or not do it at all.
- *Set aside time to get started.* Clear your calendar to do a delayed task, say from 9:00 to 11:00 on a Friday or Saturday morning, so that you can't say you don't have time to do it. Start with a "leading task," such as gathering the material needed to do the job. That builds momentum for carrying on with the rest. And peck away at small steps on what appear to be overwhelming tasks. Sometimes called the "swiss cheese method," taking small steps eats holes in the total task and makes it gradually become more manageable.
- *Make a public commitment to a completion date and promise yourself a reward when the job is done.* By announcing that you will have something done at a particular time, you create the "negative incentive" of public embarrassment for not completing the task on time. By promising yourself a reward, such as a new jacket or a night out on the town, you have a greater "positive incentive" for finishing up.

HOW TO DELEGATE ASSIGNMENTS

As the previous chapter explains, time is one of your most precious commodities. You can't do everything yourself—although it is tempting to try when people don't do things the way you would like. Many managers resist delegating, especially those who came up through the ranks and have good technical skills, because they believe they can handle most jobs better themselves. Others are unskilled at delegating —they cannot seem to plan and organize things well enough to make assignments in a timely and effective fashion. Some managers have had bad experiences delegating—they did not monitor their employees' work carefully and things went off course. Others think that explaining directions to an employee will take longer than doing the task themselves. And still others fear being outshined by their workers—these managers want to keep the credit for getting important jobs done.

Nevertheless, as a supervisor you should be a coach, not a player. You must learn to get as much pleasure from seeing employees do a first-rate job as you did when you handled the job yourself. You must enjoy teaching other people, motivating them and measuring their performance. But you can only find satisfaction in supervision and improve the likelihood of having your expectations met if you delegate assignments effectively.

TIPS FOR DELEGATING EFFECTIVELY

Assign duties to the right people. Consider employees' confidence, motivation and skill before matching them with a task. If someone seems to lack competence, start with simple, brief tasks; then gradually increase the scope of assignments.

Grant people enough authority to accomplish the delegated task on their own. Many supervisors give people the responsibility or obligation to do a job, but withhold the authority to make the decisions and take the actions necessary for carrying it out. If material and equipment are needed, the employee needs the authority to acquire the necessary resources. If help from other people is needed, the employee must have the authority to give orders and to expect them to be carried out.

A staff specialist in a bank, for example, was given the responsibility of improving customer service. But he was not given the budget to print the brochures he wanted describing the bank's services. And when he provided tellers with new "scripts" to use when dealing with customers, the tellers were lax in following them. But he had no authority to insist that they use the scripts. Although he was responsible for improving customer service, he lacked the necessary authority.

Limits of authority must be clarified as well. Good delegators tell their employees what they can and cannot do. You should explicitly tell employees what they are free to do, what you simply want to be informed about and what they must gain your approval for first.

Retain sensitive tasks yourself. Don't abdicate your responsibility. Some jobs should be done by the person in charge. Retain for yourself policy-making decisions and the handling of confidential information. Issues involving important budget and personnel matters ordinarily should not be delegated. Nevertheless, be sure to delegate some interesting, meaningful tasks along with the routine "dirty work." Morale improves greatly if you occasionally delegate a choice assignment, such as sending a worker on a field trip to visit a supplier or customer or to bring back new ideas from a conference.

Minimize "yo-yo" delegation. Employees get frustrated when a supervisor first delegates an assignment and later takes it back. This can happen when the supervisor gives poor instructions and the employee makes a mistake, resulting in the supervisor's loss of faith in the employee. It also happens when the supervisor realizes the job is more important than originally anticipated. The latter occurred when a supervisor assigned someone to improve quality controls and then learned that the company president was measuring quality in every department. The supervisor took back the assignment and irritated her employee in the process.

Make the assignments specific. Be sure your employees know what they are supposed to do, when the job should be completed, the standards by which their performance will be evaluated and what they should do if problems arise. Unless these issues are clarified ahead of time, employees will assume they know what you want—often incorrectly.

It is best to divide large jobs or projects into small segments and ask employees to report briefly to you as each part is completed. That way you can stay informed about what they are doing, feel comfortable that the project is proceeding on schedule and as expected, eliminate the possibility of someone procrastinating key tasks and provide praise or corrective feedback all along the way rather than just at the end.

When delegated assignments are completed effectively, be sure to give the employee due recognition. Even arrange a small celebration to give public credit for the accomplishment. Doing so motivates that individual, and others, to carry out future tasks with care and enthusiasm.

HOW TO
ACHIEVE GOALS
AND IMPROVE QUALITY

SETTING AND ACHIEVING GOALS

People work better when they have a goal. Zig Ziglar tells
about his friend who is a champion archer. Ziglar points out
that even if you have never before shot a bow and arrow, you
can be more accurate than his friend if you make only one
change—blindfold the archer and turn him around so he
doesn't know where his target is. No matter how skilled they
are, people shoot blindly when they don't have a clear goal.
Their efforts are scattered and accomplish little. But even
amateurs will hit the target when they know what they are
aiming for.

Setting goals is an important aspect of supervision. Yet goals
must be carefully crafted. If you want to set effective goals,
keep these considerations in mind.

Describe the desired end state or condition. Telling
employees their goal is to become better salespersons or
master carpenters gives them a life-long task, one that is never
fulfilled. Setting a goal of increasing sales 10 percent over the
last period or building an outdoor deck are tasks that can be
completed within a reasonable time.

Be clear, concise, unambiguous. Goals should mean
precisely the same thing to the supervisor and the worker.
Therefore, use concrete terms. A goal of achieving a typing
test score of 60 words a minute by August 30th is better than
one of becoming a faster typist by the end of the summer.

Specify when and how the work should be done and who will be responsible for checking accomplishment of the goal, if appropriate. Try to anticipate questions that might arise regarding the method used to achieve the goal and the quality of its performance. To reduce the likelihood of misinterpretation, add a statement such as: "The wiring department will complete 400 chassis boards by March 1st. Boards that do not pass inspection will be subtracted from the total. No overtime employment will be used. Scrap must be kept to 5 percent of total materials cost."

Set goals at three difficulty levels: routine, challenging and innovative. Routine goals are the *minimum* requirements for a position. Inform each employee that achievement of routine goals is uniformly expected.

Challenging objectives are those which add to a worker's professional expertise without changing the original job focus.

An innovative aim involves a *breakthrough* for the person and the firm. It represents an ideal to work toward.

Involve employees in goal setting. Involving people in setting their own work goals increases their acceptance or "ownership" of those goals. You might get employees to identify a reasonably challenging level of performance by asking, "How much do you think you can sell in the next three months?" Or, set a goal and then ask employees if it is reasonable. If they object, ask for a full explanation. If their concern is one you have already considered, explain why you think the goal actually can be achieved. If their objection is news to you, take it into account and reset the goal if necessary.

THE SUPERVISOR'S GUIDE

Connect goals to employees' values. A value is a deeply held belief or conviction, such as the idea that people should earn their pay or that everyone should be treated fairly. Relate goals to the underlying values or principles on which they are based. You might explain, for example, "I've tried to be as fair as possible in setting this goal," or "Achieving this goal will help you get ahead in this company." Tying goals to underlying values is especially important if the employee values the organization's purpose. If the organization provides a service that makes peoples' lives more pleasant or healthy, for example, demonstrate how achieving the goals will make a big difference to customers or clients: "Unless you deliver this promptly, people could be endangered," or "These people work very hard all year to afford this well-deserved week of leisure."

Set goals that are challenging, yet realistic. Goals can be motivating. If people accept a goal as worthwhile and realistic, they will stretch themselves to achieve it. And they will feel more gratified after achieving a challenging goal than one that is easy. Keep in mind, however, that there is a limit to how high a goal can be set. Seemingly impossible goals make workers feel their efforts are futile and reduce their motivation.

Be sure to evaluate the achievement of goals. Employees will take a goal more seriously if they know their performance will be measured. Goals set and then forgotten by a supervisor soon are ignored by workers too. Explain how achievement of the goal will be evaluated and what likely rewards are contingent upon achieving it.

Goal setting is a crucial tool for organizing and motivating employees' efforts. Use goals wisely to channel your employees' work in appropriate directions.

IMPROVING QUALITY

Most successful organizations, such as IBM, Marriott Hotels, or the Harvard Medical School, are known for producing high quality products or providing high quality services. For an organization to develop a reputation for quality, leadership must come from the top—upper management must emphasize and reward quality performance.

But quality actually gets built in where the work is done. That is where the supervisor's contribution is essential.

What can supervisors do to assure that the work for which they are responsible is of highest quality? Here are eight principles of quality improvement you can help put into action.

Prevention is superior to detection. Organizing work so that problems do not occur—and if they do occur, catching them as soon as possible—is much less expensive than detecting and correcting defects further down the line. The cost of recalling an automobile after it is sold or of correcting a data entry error after a check is issued, for example, is far greater than the cost of carefully checking that the work is done correctly the first time. Avoid, therefore, rushing people to meet a deadline if that means sacrificing quality. Quantity without quality, in the long run, is foolhardy.

Quality is conformance to requirements. Unless you establish standards for the work you supervise, people will use their own judgment to assess when they are doing quality work. You and your employees are likely to have different standards. Customers will not know what to expect. Conflicts and complaints will be frequent. Be sure to communicate clearly the precise standards your employees' work should meet.

Zero defects should be achieved. The fewer defects the better. *No* defects is best of all. With attention to quality controls, this level of performance can be achieved. Making zero defects a goal gives employees something challenging to shoot for—and when it occurs over a period of time, a cause for justifiable pride. Having zero defects enabled the United States to put astronauts on the moon. It is a key standard for making any organization competitive, either locally or internationally. Supervisors should make sure workers shoot for zero defects and receive feedback on their progress toward achieving it.

Quality is measured by the cost of nonconformance. Keep in mind, and point out to others, the hidden payoffs of high quality work. Nonconformance to quality standards may get a job done more quickly or more cheaply, but expenses will mount later through:
- Granting refunds or exchanges on poor products.
- Paying employees for doing the same job twice.
- Losing good will and repeat business.
- Paying for more quality control equipment or personnel to prevent further problems.
- Possible liability suits to recover costs incurred from the consequences of shoddy materials or workmanship.

Calculate and point out to employees the cost to your organization, and to them, of making mistakes.

Carefully select and train suppliers. Good work results only when first-rate supplies are used. Vendors of goods and services, therefore, should be selected with care. Be sure your suppliers are given specifications to assure that their input meets your requirements. Good organizations work closely with reliable suppliers over a long period of time to assure that they receive what they want when they want it.

Slogans about quality cannot do the job alone*.* Some organizations simply put up posters that read "Do it right the first time" or "Let's be error free" and believe they have a quality assurance program. If errors do not decrease, they blame employees. Such an effort is insufficient, however, and poor results should be expected. To take hold, quality controls must be built into the system.

Set objectives for achieving quality*.* Quality does not result from advice to "do your best" or to "be careful." Measurable objectives must be set. A photocopy store manager might say, "Our goal is to reduce the number of complaints from customers by half, from four to two, in the month of March." Be sure your employees have concrete quality goals to shoot for in the upcoming work period.

Reward quality performance*.* When people achieve quality performance, be sure they receive some sort of reward tied clearly to that achievement. Examples are public recognition, a cash bonus, a company-paid night out on the town, high performance appraisal ratings, promotions or compliments.

Employees do best what you expect them to do, show interest in, and reward them for. Let's put these motivators to work for quality!

HOW TO SELECT, TRAIN AND EVALUATE EMPLOYEES

CONDUCTING JOB INTERVIEWS

You are hiring a new employee. An ad in the newspaper has produced applications from a handful of qualified candidates. As a supervisor you must select from among them one that will work to achieve the company's goals and take pride in turning in a quality performance. An interview is scheduled with each applicant. How should you handle that conversation?

The questions you ask should be based on a careful *job analysis*. That is, you should first identify the knowledge, skills and attitudes a person needs to be successful in that position. Also, you need to be aware of any unusual requirements of the job. This information will determine the questions you pose in the interview.

Screening Versus Selecting

An interview has two parts. The first consists of screening. It begins with "knock-out" questions related to special job requirements. These are usually "yes-no" questions that the candidate must answer a certain way in order to be qualified.

- Are you willing to work weekends? (The job is in a restaurant, and weekend work is essential.)
- Do you wear glasses? (Government regulations require uncorrected 20-20 vision for pilots.)

- Do you know Wordstar? (The job is for a word-processing technician.)

The second part of the interview enables you to *select* from among the people qualified in all the basic ways. Here you might ask about personal qualities, school achievement, work experience, skills in dealing with people and career orientation. Some sample questions are presented in Table 2.

Questions to Avoid

It is unethical or illegal to ask about factors irrelevant to candidates' ability to perform the job in question. You would not want anyone to judge you based on the following factors, so you should avoid even asking about them in an interview. In fact, doing so could cause the candidate to file a discrimination charge with the Equal Employment Opportunity Commission (EEOC).

- *Race or color.* You *cannot* base hiring decisions on race or skin color.
- *Gender.* Unless the position is for a restroom attendant or actor, do not ask.
- *Age.* Do not ask for age or birthdate.
- *Marital status.* Do not ask if the applicant is married, single, separated, divorced, widowed or engaged.
- *Number of children or dependents.* Do not ask about applicant's family, but if the position is in childcare, you can ask about experience dealing with children.
- *National origin.* Avoid this question unless citizenship is a requirement, for example, for holding a government position.
- *Physical and mental disabilities.* You cannot ask about handicaps or disabilities, but you can ask about impairments that would interfere with ability to handle the position in question.

Table 2   Questions for Selecting Employees

Work Experience
What were your duties in your last job?
What did you like best about that job?
What did you like least?
Of what one achievement are you most proud?
What was one weakness or shortcoming in your performance?
Why did you leave that position?
Why do you want to work for this company?
What did you like about your boss in that position?
What irritated you?
How were you different from most of your co-workers there?
How were you similar?

Education
What was the highest level of education you achieved?
What subject or class did you especially like?
What subject or class did you dislike?
What were your special achievements in school?
Have you considered further schooling?
What outside-of-school training have you attended?
Describe your favorite teacher.

Career Plans
What are you looking for in a job?
What can you contribute to this company?
What are your salary requirements?
What would you like to be doing in five years? 10 years?
How satisfied are you with your present career progress?

- *Criminal record.* Ask only if the conviction would have a direct bearing on job performance; for example, candidates for a bank guard position can be asked if they have ever been convicted for a robbery offense.
- *Maiden name or previous name.* This line of questioning could be interpreted as asking for the person's nationality or marital status.

Guidelines for Beginning

Here are some suggestions for conducting the interview so that it helps you pick the right employee:

Prepare in advance. Prepare a set of questions you intend to ask everyone—some generic questions, such as those listed previously, and some "knock-out" questions based on the particular requirements of the position to be filled. Also, review each candidate's application to identify particular personal characteristics or skills you want to know more about.

Use a brief warm-up period. Conduct the interview in a private spot, and make sure you will not be interrupted. Spend the first few minutes of the interview relaxing the candidate and establishing rapport. You might talk about the candidate's trip to your site, sports, the weather or anything else that would put the person at ease.

Use a few broad, general questions. Feel free to ask some very general questions that get the candidate talking and sharing what is important to him or her. For example, you might say, "Tell me about your work history," "What was your high school like?" and "What kinds of activities do you enjoy most?"

Finally, remember to ask candidates whether they have any questions they would like to ask you!

ORIENTATION AND TRAINING

Orientation

Most large organizations have a standard orientation program to get new employees off the ground. Yet, although personnel specialists may provide much basic information, the immediate supervisor is the most important influence on new employees' attitudes and performance. Employees typically forget most of what they are told in formal orientation sessions, so it is up to you to continue the orientation process in a gradual manner.

To be sure you provide a comprehensive orientation, review the following list:

1. Greet or welcome new employee.
2. Provide brief overview of organization's purpose and history.
3. Explain overall departmental purpose, organization and relationship to other activities of the company.
4. Explain new employee's contribution to objectives of department and his or her starting assignment in broad terms.
5. Discuss job content (provide a copy of the job description, if available).
6. Explain departmental training programs and incentives, such as pay raise procedures, bonuses, awards and so forth.
7. Discuss where employee lives and transportation to and from work, parking arrangements, employee entrance and so on.
8. Explain working conditions (work hours and method for recording them; lunch hours; coffee breaks and rest periods; personal phone calls and mail; overtime policy; procedure for being paid; lockers; uniforms; equipment).

9. Explain requirements for continuation of employment (performance of duties; attendance and punctuality; handling confidential information; personal behavior; personal appearance; appearance of work area).
10. Introduce to other workers and supervisors.
11. Explain how to present complaints and suggestions for improvement.
12. Familiarize with workplace and begin on-the-job training.

On-the-Job Training

As with orientation, many companies provide classroom job training. The majority of learning, however, takes place as the work is being done at the job site. Here are some steps to keep in mind when training an employee to do an unfamiliar operation.

Define the task to be learned specifically. Provide the big picture first. What will the employee be able to do? For example, "Your job will involve preparing a rental contract for each apartment." Explain why this task is so important—who benefits and how when it is performed properly and what happens when it is not done well.

Invite two-way communication. Encourage the trainee to make comments, ask questions, and provide feedback as you go along. Find out what he or she already knows about this kind of job.

Do the training at the work site. Familiarize the trainee with the equipment, materials, tools and trade terms involved. Explain quality and quantity requirements for the job.

Demonstrate the work procedures. First, go through the job at a normal work pace. Next, go through it again at a slow pace, explaining each step. Do this a few times. Between demonstrations explain the difficult parts and those in which errors are likely to be made. Finally, go through the steps at a slow pace again, but this time have the employee explain each step and the key points to remember about each step as you go through them.

Performance tryout. Ask the employee to go slowly through the job several times, explaining each step to you. Correct any mistakes the employee makes. If necessary, do some of the complicated steps yourself the first few times. You, the supervisor, do the job at a normal pace. Have the learner do the job, gradually building up skill and speed. When the employee demonstrates the ability to do the job, put the employee on his or her own.

Follow-up. Designate who the trainee should go to for help or to ask questions. Check work periodically for quantity and quality standards, gradually decreasing inspection as performance proves adequate. Correct faulty work patterns before they become ingrained habits. Don't forget to compliment progress at every stage and maintain the employee's confidence until standards are achieved.

CONDUCTING PERFORMANCE APPRAISALS

Most employees want to know what their supervisors think of their performance. Most supervisors hate to tell them. They feel very uncomfortable providing performance appraisals because no one wants to criticize someone who is eager to be praised. And that's how many supervisors view performance appraisals. But it's a distorted view. Here, we'll provide a better way to view and handle the awkward process of performance appraisal.

Purpose of Appraisals

What is the purpose of a performance appraisal? It can achieve many purposes. A well-prepared and delivered appraisal may:

- Motivate employees by providing both positive and negative feedback on their performance.
- Encourage supervisors to observe their employees more closely, and therefore, to do a better job of coaching them.
- Help employees achieve better performance and productivity.
- Provide merit information for distributing pay raises, bonuses and promotions equitably.

Despite these worthwhile objectives, many employees view performance appraisals as "report cards" comparing them to other employees. In this context, it is not surprising that employees react defensively to suggestions for improvement. Yet all employees must be informed of the areas in which they can improve.

A Two-Way Discussion

The key to making performance appraisals worthwhile is transforming them from a one-way evaluation into a two-way discussion, a process that begins by notifying employees in advance that the appraisal meeting is coming up. They should be encouraged to prepare to bring to the supervisor's attention their major accomplishments for the past work period and how they hope to improve their contributions in the coming period.

At the meeting, the supervisor might start the discussion by putting the employee at ease and then asking, "As you look at it, how are things going on the job?"

The supervisor should be sure to allow the employee to identify positive contributions by asking something like, "What pleases you most about what you've done during the past year?"

Ask the employee if there are any barriers to doing the job well, and if so, for suggestions for overcoming those barriers. This is the point at which concerns about unnecessary red tape and bureaucratic procedures might come up. You can explain why some controls are necessary or solicit ways to reduce or even eliminate what is unnecessary.

Be an active listener. Paraphrase what employees say to indicate that you are genuinely concerned that they are getting through to you, and that you understand the message correctly. Keep an open mind—let your subsequent remarks in the performance appraisal reflect what you learned in this exchange, rather than simply saying what you had planned regardless of what the employee has told you.

Supervisors also should summarize how they perceive the employee's overall performance, avoiding comparisons to other people. In this statement, emphasize desirable behaviors to continue in the future. In addition, point out one or two "opportunities for improvement"—this puts the emphasis on future achievement rather than past failures. Phrase suggested improvements as work behaviors, not as personality traits. Translate them into specific goals rather than vague directions. For example, if you want an employee to reduce materials waste, set a precise, acceptable level of scrap and identify how, when and by whom it will be measured. Develop a concrete plan for improving performance in specific ways for the coming year.

If possible, separate the performance appraisal from any salary review. If company policy allows, discuss salary increases a few weeks after the performance appraisal session. Of course, salary decisions should be linked to the results of the performance appraisals. But if the performance appraisal focuses on money, very little attention will be given to performance improvement. Employees get emotional about money, and when it is at stake, all else can momentarily become secondary.

A natural closing topic is what the long-range future might hold for the employee. Ambitious individuals want to know about possibilities for advancement. Security-conscious employees want reassurance that their positions are secure. Whenever possible, close on a constructive, encouraging note, such as, "I'm confident that we'll follow up on the plans we've made, and the upcoming year will be an outstanding one for you."

HOW TO DEVELOP EMPLOYEE POTENTIAL AND SATISFACTION

MOTIVATING YOUR EMPLOYEES

The subtitle of this section is misleading. People are already motivated. Motivation is inborn. Without motivation, people would never get out of bed.

Harnessing Inborn Motivations
A supervisor's challenge lies not in motivating people, but in harnessing the motivations they already have, in getting them to expend their effort to accomplish organizational goals and to produce quality work, as discussed in the previous chapters.

What are inborn motivations? Psychologist Abraham Maslow identified the most basic ones. He pointed out that all human motivators, or needs, are innate but that each comes to the fore or predominates in a person's life only if more basic motivators are satisfied. Hierarchically, from the most basic to the more complex, human motives include:
- Physiological – the need for food, shelter and sexual gratification.
- Safety – protection from the environment or people.
- Social – the need for love, affection and sense of belonging.
- Esteem – the desire for self-respect and the good opinion of others.
- Self-fulfillment – the need to gain satisfaction from one's work, to realize the world values the contribution.

Do you find each of these needs in yourself? Do they influence why you work?

Note that if one of the more basic needs is unfulfilled, the higher level needs decrease in importance. That is, people who are hungry or homeless struggle just to survive and probably care little about social status or the society in which they live.

Here's another way to explain motivation. Some people think what people talk about most at work—money, company policies, or their lousy boss—is what really "matters" or what motivates them. This isn't true, especially if people are *complaining*. What *bothers* people about a job is not the same as what *motivates* them to do an outstanding job. Frederick Hertzberg called what dissatisfies people "hygiene" factors and what satisfies people "motivators."

When hygiene factors are inadequate, people grumble and feel unmotivated. Hygiene factors include:

- salary
- working conditions
- relationships with co-workers
- job status
- job security
- company policies and administration
- supervision

Think about your own work. When you feel you are getting less than your fair share or less than what you need in any of the areas listed above, do you feel *dissatisfied*?

You probably do.

Now, if you receive an improvement or increase in any of

these factors, would that *motivate* you to try doing your job much better than you are doing it now?

Probably not.

Next, consider Hertzberg's ideas about what makes a job motivating to people:
- Receiving feedback about the results being achieved.
- Serving a client or customer directly.
- Learning new skills and growing mentally.
- Doing a unique, specialized job.
- Having freedom to schedule their own work.
- Having control, or being able to obtain resources when needed.
- Having direct communication authority—access to users of work output.
- Having personal accountability—clearly earning praise or blame depending on how work is done.

Would you try harder if your job had more of these qualities? Hertzberg thinks you would. He calls these "qualities of an enriched job" and claims that they hook peoples' innate motivation and direct that energy into quality work performance.

Consider whether the jobs you supervise have these qualities. If they lack any of them, can you increase them? If you can, you have a tool for harnessing motivation.

Goal Setting
Another important tool is *goal setting*. When aiming to achieve a goal they value–especially one that is challenging, specific and realistic–people put forth greater effort than when they are just told to "do their best."

Do the employees you supervise work to achieve clear goals? If not, goal setting could be a potent motivating force.

Reinforcement

Another tool is *reinforcement*, or rewarding desired behavior. People tend to increase performance of behaviors that bring desired consequences and to avoid behaviors followed by undesired consequences. Thus, praising or providing material rewards for the kind of work you want people to do motivates them to continue working that way. Ignoring or punishing people when they do what you want decreases their motivation to do that kind of work. Do you "stroke" or provide incentive rewards when—and *only when*—people do good work? If so, you are using reinforcement as a motivator. Does everyone receive the same rewards at work no matter how well they perform? If so, you are neglecting reinforcement as a motivation tool. This approach to motivation is so important, we will discuss it in greater detail in the next section.

BEHAVIOR MODIFICATION TECHNIQUES

Suppose you want to change someone's performance at work. Usually, you simply request or demand what you want, and people do what you ask. At other times, however, change doesn't come so easily. Old habits are hard to break.

Think of yourself. We bet you occasionally disobey your own orders! Perhaps you want to stop smoking, start exercising, eat fewer desserts, or quit yelling at your kids. Yet, before you know it, you break your resolution and do exactly what you told yourself not to do.

How can you overcome this resistance to change? Techniques

of *behavior modification* have had remarkable success. Here are the steps involved:

Set standards for job performance. A precise description of the desired behavior, phrased to enable you to measure how much or how well people are doing it, is crucial.

Occasionally, the goal is to improve what is already occurring. If so, you should first measure the status quo—called the baseline figure—and then set a reasonable target for improvement. Perhaps you want a group to produce more, to save money on expenses, to have fewer rejections, or come up with more suggestions for improvement. You would first measure how the employees are doing now in that regard, thereby establishing a baseline, before setting your goal for change.

Agree on rewards. The key to behavior modification is rewarding or reinforcing people when they perform in the desired way. This reward need not involve simply giving more money in the forms of bonuses, profit sharing or salary increases. Financial rewards, of course, usually do motivate, but other forms of reinforcement also prove very effective.

Before implementing any reward system, be sure the employee perceives the designated reward as valuable. People work only for what they themselves genuinely want. Also consider whether you want *individuals* or *groups* to earn the reward. If you allow individuals to earn their own rewards, you encourage competition and initiative. If you give rewards to groups, you encourage cooperation and teamwork. Each approach has its dangers: individual rewards sometimes lead people to sabotage their competitors' efforts; group rewards sometimes tempt people to "coast" or "free-ride" on others' efforts. A combination of individual and group rewards is best.

Emery Air Freight, for example, uses large containers to transfer small packages to and between airlines in order to cut handling and delivery times. They want these containers used 90 percent of the time, and the workers polled thought they used them about this often. Actual measurements indicated the baseline figure was closer to 45 percent. So, management developed a checklist on which dock workers indicated each time they used a container. Workers totaled their own results at the end of each shift. Supervisors provided positive reinforcement by praising any improvement in employee performance. If improvement was minimal, the employees were lauded for keeping an honest record of container usage. As a result, in 80 percent of the offices where the technique was employed, the use of containers rose from 45 percent to 95 percent. When the whole company shifted to this system, it saved $650,000 a year.

MANAGING INADEQUATE PERFORMANCE

Despite your efforts to motivate and reward, some employees continually perform their tasks in a sub-par manner or display behavior that is unacceptable. An employee repeatedly comes to work late. An employee gets less work done than you expect. An employee's work has too many errors.

When people perform inadequately, something needs to be done. Berating such employees or urging them to improve is usually ineffective. The problem simply continues. Why? Perhaps the worker lacks what it takes to succeed. Then again, perhaps you aren't handling the problem appropriately.

Below is a systematic approach to dealing with people who perform inadequately. Consider each step carefully—be sure you are part of the solution, not part of the problem.

Define and communicate what acceptable performance is. People should not be blamed for not doing what they do not know they are supposed to do. That's obvious, of course. But you may not realize that you aren't communicating your expectations clearly. Say you tell someone, "I expect you to be at work at 8:00 a.m." To you that's perfectly clear—it means being at the work station and in action at that time. To the employee, however, that message may mean coming in the door at 8:00. Using the restroom and getting equipment or a cup of coffee might take another few minutes, so actual work does not start until 8:10 or 8:15. You consider such behavior inadequate and a direct violation of your instructions. The worker, however, believes he or she is doing nothing wrong. So, as you can see, establishing clear standards comes first.

Detect deviations from acceptable performance. The more people get away with what is not acceptable, the more that lower level of work becomes a "norm" and gradually replaces what is desired. Stay on top of what people are doing. Manage by walking around. Do not be aloof from the work site, thus tacitly implying that "anything goes" because "nobody knows" what is going on. Also, when you see something wrong, bring it up as soon as possible.

Let the responsible employee know what you have observed. Because confronting a poor performer can be difficult, these precautions should be kept in mind:
1. *Confront the employee privately, not in front of other people.* Also, be sure time is available for a full discussion. This makes the worker less likely to "lose

face" in front of others or try to "save face" by reacting defensively to your message.

2. *Try to relax.* Take a deep breath and count to 10 before beginning the discussion, especially if you feel angry about what you have observed. A confrontation need not be a dressing down, an argument or a debate. It should be a problem-solving session in which both parties try rationally to remedy an unsatisfactory situation.

3. *Get to the central purpose of your meeting quickly.* Small talk is appropriate for other kinds of meetings, but the serious purpose of this particular conversation should be immediately apparent.

4. *Do not be apologetic about the need for the meeting.* Avoid starting with "I hate to say this, but. . ." Everyone in an organization has a responsibility to both co-workers and the people they serve to do the job appropriately. Just say what you have detected and let the worker correct you if you are wrong.

5. *Consider and discuss the possible cause of the problem.* Keep in mind that performance problems may exist for a variety of reasons, although we often *assume* laziness or hostility are the cause. Causes may exist within the employee, the job, the organization or the supervisor:

    a. The employee: physical ailments, family disputes, alcohol abuse or lack of up-to-date knowledge.

    b. The job: fatigue, boredom, demands of co-workers ("don't raise the quota"), or ergonomic problems (such as glare from a computer screen), even pollution (headache from mold allergy).

    c. The organization: lack of proper tools, toleration of slow performance or no incentive or reward provided for working faster.

    d. The supervisor: failure to give clear instructions, failure to give feedback about rate of performance or inappropriate supervisory style—new worker isn't getting close supervision or experienced worker is being suffocated by incessant inspections.

Set improvement goals. Explicitly state the level of performance you expect for the person's work to be considered acceptable. Be sure you identify the date by which that level should be achieved.

Establish an action plan. Deal with the cause of poor performance. If you do not want the problem to be repeated, you must address the cause. Action plans that are often used include:
- Closer supervision.
- Job reassignment or transfer.
- Referral to employee assistance program for counseling.
- A change or increase in employee incentives.
- Lower performance standards for a while.

Schedule a "follow-up on progress" meeting or establish another way to monitor the worker's progress towards achieving the established goals.

BOOSTING EMPLOYEE MORALE

Should you invest effort to make employees happy?

Some bosses don't care. They say work output is all that matters. Granted, satisfied workers do not necessarily work harder. But other benefits do accrue to supervisors who attend to employee morale. Satisfied workers are more likely to:
- Help co-workers with job-related problems.
- Accept orders without a fuss.

- Help keep the work area clean and uncluttered.
- Conserve company supplies, parts and funds.
- Make constructive suggestions for improvement.
- Speak well about the department or company to outsiders.
- Come to work regularly and remain with the company.
- Have good safety records.

Because good morale has been shown to have these and other benefits, supervisors should do what they can to improve it. Here are some qualities known to increase job satisfaction.

Mentally challenging work. Doing only repetitive, routine work bores and frustrates most people. Supervisors should adjust jobs so that they are challenging enough to hold peoples' attention. Often this is done by assigning a wider range of responsibilities to people doing highly specialized work.

Reasonable physical demands. Doing work that taxes one's physical limits, such as driving a truck for many hours at a stretch or operating a noisy machine all day, also is frustrating. Supervisors should recognize and try to alleviate unreasonable physical demands. People cannot work beyond their physical capacity for very long before they feel negative psychological and physical consequences. Allowing employees to take breaks when they feel they are needed, for example, increases satisfaction and reduces job "burn out."

Contact with end user. Working in anonymity, making something or preparing a service and then sending out what's produced without any personal contact with its recipient is not satisfying. Arranging for employees to talk with the people who use what they produce (such as the restaurant patrons who eat what a cook prepares or the operators who use a machine repaired by an electrician) adds to the satisfaction of those employees.

Meaningful rewards. When exceptional performance makes little difference in the rewards an employee receives, satisfaction goes down. Meaningful rewards are fair and informative and meet a need. A fair reward is commensurate with what was done—such as a day off as a reward for working overtime. An informative reward indicates precisely what was done—such as being given an award for having the fewest absences in the department over the last year. A reward that is meaningful is one the recipient would value—such as a gift certificate from a nursery to a person who loves gardening.

Contribution to self-esteem. Dissatisfied people feel that they are not valued or doing valuable work. Supervisors should communicate to workers that what they do is important and appreciated. Supervisors should treat people as worthwhile individuals. Also, by rolling up their sleeves and pitching in to help out with the work to be done, supervisors indicate that the work and the workers' good will are valued.

Maintain open communication. Satisfaction is increased if employees feel their supervisor will listen to what is on their minds and take it seriously. Employees may have a complaint about what has been going on, a suggestion for improving procedures or a request for a small favor. If the supervisor is available to hear what employees have to say, considers it carefully, and gives a reasoned response, employees' job satisfaction will grow.

Allow for participative management. People feel more satisfied if they are consulted before decisions that will affect their work lives are made. Employees prefer being given a chance to provide information and express opinions about matters on which they have first-hand knowledge. To increase satisfaction when problems arise or changes are being considered, ask workers for their input.

Be flexible. People become dissatisfied when they are forced to conform to inconvenient rules that are not justified. For example, many organizations are now installing "flextime," programs that allow adjustments in work schedules so that workers can meet their personal and family obligations more effectively. Flextime programs usually result in greater job satisfaction because employees feel the organization is doing what it reasonably can to accommodate their needs.

Positive morale provides a good foundation for everything else that goes on at work. You can do a great deal to raise your employees' morale—and thereby make things more pleasant for yourself too.

REDUCING JOB STRESS

Human beings need a reasonable level of challenge. When faced with demands, the mind and body naturally respond—physical and mental effort are expended. If demands are relentless and needed relief isn't available, people feel overloaded. Stress builds up, and eventually people feel "burned out." On the other hand, if work demands too little, it becomes boring, and eventually people "rust out."

When demands and effort are well matched, people feel in the "flow"—they are optimally satisfied and productive.

Supervisors want to provide for others and experience for themselves this well-balanced, appropriate amount of stress.

However, people do not necessarily feel the same amount of stress from a given situation. Giving a speech, for example, is very stressful to some people and hardly stressful at all to others. Moreover, some people can handle more stressful responsibilities than others.

Managing stress at work, therefore, isn't easy. People must be placed in jobs that suit them, and job demands must be adapted to suit the stress tolerance of the people who fill them.

We all know that illness or loss provoke stress. Many causes of stress at work, however, are subtle and easily overlooked by supervisors. Here are some stress factors you should watch for:

Ambiguous directions. When people don't know exactly what they are supposed to do, they are likely to feel uncertain and anxious. They don't know if they are doing too much or too little, if what they are doing is right or wrong, if they are stepping on someone's toes or letting work fall between the cracks. Being sure people can get their questions answered at work helps reduce stress.

Conflicting demands. Many people report to more than one person at work. Stress builds up when these superiors give conflicting instructions. For example, a secretary who takes assignments from several executives may be given two "top priority" assignments on the same day. Another example is a company in which top management has one policy and a local manager has another. The company president gave a speech insisting that high quality standards always be maintained, but a district manager rewarded only high quantity output, regardless of quality. Company supervisors felt caught in the middle. If people you supervise are in such a bind, develop a procedure for talking over the conflicting demands, one that provides an opportunity for everyone involved to be satisfied.

Too much work or too little work. People feel stressed if they are overloaded with work, especially if it cannot all be done within the normal work week. They feel exhausted at the end of the day and worry about the consequences of having a pile of "unfinished business." Remarkably, people also feel stressed if they do not have enough to do. They worry about job security, about being perceived as lazy, and about not pulling their weight. Be sure the people you supervise have a reasonable amount of work to do.

Technostress or computer shock. People who have a strong need for personal relationships but work primarily with machines can feel isolated and dehumanized at work. These employees need to be given a wider range of tasks to do, preferably tasks that involve contact with people, or be transferred to another job. People who spend long hours in front of a computer terminal may experience aching muscles and a detached, glassy-eyed look. They need a chance for reasonable rest periods and, whenever possible, rotation to other kinds of assignments.

Dealing with seemingly hopeless problems. People feel stressed when they must deal all day with problems they can do little about. Attendants working with chronically ill people, guards working with hardened criminals, social workers who care for children of abusive parents, and others who feel like they are swimming upstream and making little headway can build up stress. They need to be reassured that they are making slow, steady progress and that their efforts are recognized and appreciated.

Lack of positive feedback and appreciation. Many supervisors assume that people do not need to be told they are doing a good job. They feel the worker's achievements are obvious and do not need to be mentioned. Also, many people perform jobs whose quality is not apparent. Those who carry out only a small part of a larger product or service—a welder in an automobile assembly plant or a data entry clerk in a hospital records room, for example—receive only minimal indication that their work is worthwhile. This lack of recognition causes stress. These employees, too, need to be reassured that they are making a difference and that their efforts are recognized and appreciated.

Conflict and negative competition. People feel stress if there are frequent quarrels among co-workers, even if they themselves are not directly involved. They also feel stressed if people at work are placed in competition with each other–such as in sales contests–and unfair tactics are used (people steal customers from each other's territories, for example). Supervisors in such situations must be peacemakers and referees, making sure that matters are addressed and handled fairly.

Daily hassles and ongoing contact with stress carriers. When flexible action is stifled in a bureaucratic organization, people feel stressed. Examples of stifled actions are having to fill out excessive forms, being unable to see the boss when needed, being asked to work late at the last minute, having a $20 purchase request denied, and receiving a parking ticket from a company security officer. Also, stress can be contagious. Having to work alongside someone who is perpetually depressed, anxious, perfectionistic or indecisive is stressful. Coping with that individual's excessive needs may add an intolerable burden. Supervisors should make every effort to rearrange things or to remove stress-provoking stimuli from their employees' work environments.

HOW TO MANAGE CONFLICT BETWEEN EMPLOYEES

CONDITIONS THAT FOSTER CONFLICT

Conflict between people at work is virtually inevitable.
Several work conditions, however, actually foster conflict.

Competition for limited resources. When people are set
against each other to obtain limited rewards—what one wins
another loses—conflicts are likely. Such a situation can arise,
for example, if only a certain amount of money is available for
pay increases and co-workers know they are competing with
each other for a larger slice of that pie.

Differences in values and goals. People in different
organizational departments have different interests and
different preferences and, therefore, are likely to be in conflict.
Marketing, for example, wants a variety of products that meet
customers' desires and are delivered whenever they are
ordered. Manufacturing, on the other hand, prefers to produce
a few standardized products at a predictable volume. Conflict
between people from these departments is very likely.

Solving problems in different ways. Business problems,
unlike chemical formulas, can be solved in several ways,
which gives rise to conflict. For example, if costs must be cut,
one person might recommend cutting people, another cutting
equipment orders, another cutting travel expenses, another
cutting advertising costs, and so on.

Expressing natural aggression. Dealing with frustration by
building up and expressing angry feelings seems wired into
our nervous systems. That built-up energy is sometimes
harnessed to achieve constructive ends, but sometimes it is
used simply to lash out at people during a conflict. Many
people believe no one should ever get angry, so when someone
erupts, conflict exists.

ADVANTAGES AND DISADVANTAGES OF CONFLICT

Conflict in itself is neither good nor bad—it just is. What
people *do* when conflict exists determines whether it leads to
positive or negative ends.

Advantages
Without conflict, nothing would change. If you are dissatisfied, nothing will be done unless you tell someone how you
feel.

Conflict can help people grow. If you are using an ineffective
or wrong procedure, you will never learn a better way unless
someone levels with you and risks conflict.

On the other hand, if someone complains although you're
doing just fine, defending your viewpoint against an objection
helps you to understand and explain it better.

Conflicts make life interesting. Lively discussions about
differences of opinion keep work from being boring and
monotonous. A roomful of "yes" men is soporific.

Conflict strengthens unity. People never know how strong
their relationship is until they have had a fight. After getting

what they felt off their chest, they know their respect for each other is strong enough to withstand open disagreement, and they have greater faith that their relationship will last through "thick and thin."

Disadvantages

Prolonged conflict deteriorates physical and mental health. People who frequently do not get along with others at work experience a great deal of stress. They worry, their muscles tense up, their blood pressure rises and eventually they become ill.

Prolonged conflict can divert time, energy and resources away from more important goals, such as making a profit. People who must spend hours documenting that their ideas are worthwhile or that they are doing their work use energy to deal with a conflict instead of to achieve more basic organizational goals. Moreover, conflict is damaging when employees spend time planning to distort information, to strike or to sabotage a plant because they are at odds with their organization's labor-management policies.

PREVENTING CONFLICT FROM GROWING

What can a supervisor do to prevent conflict from getting out of hand? Realizing that employees will feel dissatisfied from time to time and will have gripes to air, supervisors should keep these suggestions in mind:

Take complaints seriously. Even if you have a million other things on your mind, you have heard the gripe a million times before, or you think a complaint is trivial, take it seriously. Employees occasionally make mountains out of molehills because something minor *symbolizes* something really important to them. For example, an employee complained that his raise was $5.00 less a month than someone else's. The supervisor laughed and said he should take his complaint to the Salvation Army. That worker complained to his shop steward, who took it to the officers of the company. Many meetings ensued that could have been avoided had the supervisor taken the complaint seriously, found out what it meant to the worker, and obtained an explanation through informal channels when it was first presented.

Hear out the complaint and get all sides of the story. You are acting in part as a counselor when you hear employees' complaints. Sometimes the real concern lies deeper than is first apparent. Someone's request for a transfer may boil down to an unwillingness to work with another employee. Someone complaining about a stolen tool may have mislaid it by mistake. Someone who complains about an unfriendly co-worker may have given the other person justifiable reasons for being unfriendly. Always hear all sides to a complaint, in depth, before jumping to conclusions about it.

Be fair and explain reasons for your decisions. Take both sides of any dispute into account and deal with them objectively. Before rendering any decision, reiterate the points made on both sides of an argument. Identify the *principle* underlying what you recommend, such as fairness to all, worker safety, justice or compromise. Don't say, "That's my decision, period!" Always be willing to explain your thinking.

BUILDING TEAM SPIRIT

Many supervisors these days are put in charge of "autono-mous" work groups. They lead people doing highly interdependent work. Everyone must cooperate and share responsibility for getting the group's task done.

Cooperation is a fragile quality, however. People placed together in a work group will not necessarily care about each other or pitch in to help one another. In fact, they can easily slip into distrust, conflict and competition. Supervisors must carefully nurture team spirit by being mindful of those factors that enhance group unity.

Proximity. Be sure people in the group are situated within easy reach of each other. Also try to make alterations in the physical environment to separate your group from other units, so your group is clearly seen as a distinct entity. Proximity to each other, and separation from other groups, increase a group's sense of unity.

Identification. Give your group some unique characteristics, such as its own name, logo, saying or uniform—any kind of "flag" to identify with and rally behind.

Common Ground. Assemble persons who are already alike, or remind them of the things they all have in common, such as similar basic values or a common professional role. Remember, "birds of a feather flock together."

Connect Individual and Group Needs. Help members identify the individual needs they will satisfy through participation in group efforts. Remind them that pay, promotion, time off, recognition or whatever they want comes primarily from group results. Be sure the organization awards incentives on the basis of group, not individual, performance, and everyone understands that payoffs are yielded by what the group does.

Also, keep score of the group's achievements and let the group know how well it is doing vis-a-vis other groups in the organization.

Sacrifice for the Group. Ironically, the more people do for their group, the more loyal to it they feel. If we contribute our time and effort to a group, we develop a "stake" in that group's success. In other words, our personal sacrifice only makes sense if the group prevails. If the group fails, our efforts are rendered fruitless. So the more we sacrifice, the more the group's success matters to us. If your people have to go out of their way for the group, they will become more personally committed to it.

Set Goals That Foster Group Success. When a group meets its objectives and its members feel successful, their appetite for further success is enhanced. Each success makes high quality work more desirable.

Help your group set clear, challenging, achievable goals. Goals should be neither unreasonably easy or hard. The goals become standards of excellence for all group activities, so they should not be boring or overwhelming. Change goals that appear too difficult. The warmest group pride comes from living up to reasonable expectations, not from failing impossibly difficult ends. Goals are also important because the group cannot feel successful if its members are uncertain about whether they have reached the group's objective or which way they must turn to get there.

Foster individual success. Give members assignments that suit their abilities and offer them a sense of competence. Members who think they are less competent develop more concern about their personal failures. A supervisor can, therefore, enhance members' desire for group success by helping them perform well in their own jobs and by telling them they have done well when that is the case. Do not scold or ridicule anyone publicly. Avoid the fear of failure and the subsequent tendency to evade challenges.

Emphasize responsibility for the group's fate. Make sure members understand what their individual contribution is to the final product of the whole group and that their work is valued. Emphasize that each group member depends on the work of others for the group to complete its task. Members who know that the group depends on their efforts will want to improve the quality of their work.

People with a central group role, rather than a peripheral one, develop a greater sense of group responsibility. People perceive themselves as being more central when the group is smaller. So if your your group becomes too large, break it up into smaller units.

Challenging the Process. Encourage talk in group meetings about how the group's performance can be improved and how boring parts of the daily job can be made more interesting.

Stress pride in the group. Tell people you are proud of what they have accomplished. Encourage veteran group members to talk about why they feel proud to be a group member. Publicly affirm and recognize group accomplishments, as well as the contributions of individuals to group success.

HOW TO APPROACH AND RESOLVE PROBLEMS

Supervisors try to organize activities within their areas so that everything runs smoothly. But nothing is ever as simple or as predictable as we would like. Frequently a gap exists between what we want to happen and what is actually occurring.

Many problems appear insoluble at first. They seem to yield only headaches for the supervisor. Two of your people quit during a hiring freeze. Maybe you are asked to cut your budget by 20 percent although it is already "fat free." Perhaps you are expected to install a new piece of equipment in an already overcrowded work space. Your company is moving to a new building, and you are asked to help design the layout. All these situations call for solutions that do not readily come to mind. They require creativity.

USING THE CREATIVE APPROACH

Some people believe that you are either born with creativity or you don't have it at all. That's not so. Everyone can be creative, but it must be released and harnessed. Here are some techniques for putting your creative problem-solving ability to use.

Overcome rigid mental sets. We develop habits or mental sets for perceiving familiar things around us. Being creative involves breaking those habits—seeing and using things in new ways. Have you ever wanted to jot someone a note when you didn't have a pad on hand? An uncreative person gives up at that point. A creative person looks around for something to write on—perhaps a deposit slip from a checkbook, a newspaper page not filled with print, a section of a paper bag or the back of an envelope. When you break your mental set for familiar objects so that you can use them in a new way, you are being creative. Many profitable ideas come this way.

Crown Zellerbach, the forest products company, for example, used to throw away the waste from its paper processing operations until someone creatively saw that the shavings could be formed into pellets and sold as kitty litter. Unfortunately, the company later learned that cats picked up a fine black dust from the product and tracked it all over the house. However, another firm, Tradewell Industries, bought all 4.3 million pounds of the kitty litter inventory and resold it to racetracks and horse farms as a substitute for sawdust. Breaking their mental sets for how something should be used was profitable for both companies.

Be curious and study problems. Creativity emerges from asking questions—from inquiring why certain procedures are followed, how pieces of equipment work, why they don't work, how they are fixed and so on. The creative supervisor is always trying to understand how things are currently being done, why that method is being used, what problems exist and what other methods have been considered. For example, an office supervisor in a plumbing supply company helped the company develop a new mechanism to prevent leaky toilets after he asked many questions about the common leaks the company was experiencing. His approach used water pressure to replace the troublesome floating bulb arrangement found in most toilets. [1]

---

[1] Andrew J. BuBrin, The Practice of Supervision, (2nd ed.), Plano, TX: Business Publications, 1987, p. 124.

Practice brainstorming. The worst enemy of creativity is criticism. If people fear being ridiculed, they will not suggest novel ideas, or even think of them. Brainstorming stimulates creativity by completely separating the development of ideas from the evaluation of them. Therefore, when tackling a difficult problem, on your own or with other people, throw out all possible ideas for solving it and don't allow any criticism until all ideas have been presented. Usually it takes only five minutes of brainstorming for fresh ideas to be proposed. (But you will be amazed how hard it is for some people to hold off being critical for even that short period of time!)

Use an idea log. Keep a pocket-sized notebook with you at all times for jotting down creative ideas that come to mind. Ideas may pop into your mind just before you fall asleep, while you are driving or even in the midst of a boring meeting. Be sure to capture them on paper—otherwise, they are easily forgotten and lost.

Your notebook can also be used for brainstorming. At the top of a page just write , "How can I. . .? and insert the problem you are working on. Jot down whatever ideas come to mind. Then go back to that page at other times—at least once a day— and attack the problem again. Within a few days you will have the ideas needed to solve your problem.

Establish a place for creativity. Many people have a favorite spot or activity they use to loosen up their minds for creative problem-solving. Identify where and when it is best for you to be creative, and protect it; that is, when problems arise, be sure to allot ample time for being in that spot or engaging in that activity.

Borrow creative ideas. You do not have to come up with all the creative ideas you need on your own. New solutions for the kinds of problems you face at work are being developed

every day. Many find their way into print—in books, news-
letters and magazines—or are presented in talks and tapes at
seminars. Read widely, talk to others in positions similar to
your own, and take advantage of training opportunities.
Benefit from the creative thinking of others!

INTELLIGENT PROBLEM SOLVING

Now that you know how to approach problems creatively, use
the logical series of steps that follow to solve the problems.

Find the problem. Sometimes problems are thrust in your
lap—a shipment is lost or an employee comes to work drunk.
Other problems are actively "found." Perhaps you learn that
your company is "in play" and likely to be bought by a larger
firm. If you wait for the problem to occur, you may not be
able to respond effectively. Instead, consider it a problem you
want to address now, before things get out of hand. That is,
you want to anticipate the consequences of a buy out and be
prepared to deal with them. Find the problem and begin
investigating it—say by asking your boss how you can best
prepare for it or by reading a book to learn what commonly
occurs in mergers and buy outs. Smart supervisors look for
problems rather than wait to be struck by them.

Diagnose the problem. Finding out what may have caused the
problem you are facing is the next step. Some problems are
programmed—a procedure already exists that directs how the
problem should be handled. Examples of programmed
problems are how much postage to put on a letter, how much
employees should be paid for overtime or whether smoking is
allowed in a work area. Solving programmed problems simply
involves finding out the suitable regulation.

Other, *nonprogrammed* problems are unique—simple solutions do not exist for them. You must devise your own. In these cases, you first should gather as much information as possible about the circumstances surrounding the problem. If, for example, you learn your production or service is behind schedule, it is tempting to blame your workers and assume that they are lazy or irresponsible. Don't assume—investigate. Other possible reasons could include unclear instructions or inadequate equipment. Find out the cause.

Another part of diagnosis is identifying constraints. Are funds available to repair or replace your equipment? Do union regulations restrict making a personnel change? Must you report what occurred to your boss or to a customer? What rules and restrictions might limit your response?

Develop alternative solutions. Before assuming you know how to deal with the problem or giving up on it, consider your options. Actively list them in your mind. Often they range from one end of a continuum to another. If an employee asks for a day off during a busy period, you can grant the request, you can say no, or you can do something in between. For example, you can compromise and agree to a smaller amount of time off; you can schedule another time when the work can be made up; you can ask the employee to arrange with other workers to assume responsibilities; you can hire a temporary worker; you can offer to help the employee accomplish what he or she wants to do that day without taking time off; and so on.

Generating alternative solutions is the most creative part of problem solving. Effective supervisors often think of the one additional alternative that best handles the problem. Less effective supervisors stop with the first approach that comes to mind.

Evaluate alternative solutions. Identify what is desired in an optimal solution. Use those criteria to evaluate your alternatives, and choose the solution you prefer. In the case of the request for time off, your criteria might include that the work should be done, the employee should feel that the solution is reasonable, the cost of whatever solution is adopted should be less than the cost of the employee's absence or what the employee's work earns for the company that day. Above all, the solution you devise should be one you would be willing to apply in similar situations; that is, it should be a precedent you are willing to live with. Consider each option in the light of such standards.

Select the best solution. Decide which alternative best meets all your criteria. If none do, explain your concerns to the employee and ask if he or she can suggest yet another solution. If more than one option seems acceptable, you might offer the employee or anyone else involved (such as your boss or the other members of the work team) a choice. People accept decisions better if they have a hand in devising or choosing them.

Implement the solution. Develop a plan for carrying out your plan. Be sure every step is well understood. Since the solution is an exception to the usual way of handling things, it must be carefully spelled out.

Include some means for checking whether what you decided is actually being done as planned and how well it turns out. If difficulties arise, corrective action may be needed.

As we said at the start, few things work out exactly as planned. So, a "solution" may leave you with yet another problem on your hands. If it does, simply go back through the steps outlined in this section. Remember, challenges make life interesting!

HOW TO HANDLE COMPANY POLITICS

Most supervisors would prefer to think that good work speaks for itself. Unfortunately, this policy is naive. Anyone out in the work force for a while soon learns that many factors other than ability or effort influence who obtains desired rewards and who achieves career advancement. Frankly, people rarely succeed on merit alone. Company politics are a fact of life.

"Politics" sounds like a dirty word, a self-serving practice that should apply only in public elections. Politics exist, however, in every organization and need not be unethical. Sensible supervisors simply learn to live with and master them. What we mean by politics are methods for gaining favor, advancing your career, or gaining power other than through merit or luck.

Politics need not be merely self-serving. A supervisor who uses a personal relationship with his or her boss to obtain funds for replacing an unsafe machine, for example, is using politics for a worthwhile end.

INCREASING YOUR POLITICAL CLOUT

Form a good personal relationship with your immediate supervisor. People have more power as they ascend the company hierarchy. Being human, they tend to use their power more to help people they like than people they dislike. How might you nurture your relationship with your boss? Besides doing a good job, you might:

- Ask him or her to lunch.
- Remember a birthday or anniversary with a card or gift.
- Help out with personal errands, such as assisting on moving day or providing a lift to the auto repair shop.

Help your boss look good to top management. Your boss is as eager to improve his or her standing as you are. If your boss learns about your good words, he or she is likely to reciprocate by elevating your evaluation or reputation in the organization.

Take problems away from your boss. Make a conscious effort to solve problems for your boss rather than merely presenting your boss with new problems to solve. And, if you handle a problem that might otherwise have gone to your boss, be sure to make that known.

Compliment your boss. Most people focus primarily on what their boss thinks of them. They forget that their boss is also human, has an ego, and wants to be regarded highly. Compliments provide recognition for work done well, and everyone appreciates that.

Listen to your boss. Showing your boss that you take seriously what he or she says promotes your relationship. Nod, smile and show enthusiasm when your boss is making a point; take notes at meetings; ask for suggestions and then follow them; and even listen thoughtfully when the boss shares a personal problem.

Create your own job. Do something so important for your organization that you are given control of that operation. Many a company division or government agency began with a project handled by one individual. As the project proves successful and important, more people may be hired to carry it out. For example, an assistant data entry supervisor identified a new kind of client for her company's information processing services. Because the supervisor did such a good job, the client began recommending her firm to others in that business. Soon she was appointed head of a new unit which handled that type of account.

Collect and cash in on IOUs. When you do an important favor for someone of higher rank at work, you have an implicit IOU—that individual owes you a comparable favor. If you work overtime or perform tasks not expected of you to assure that work goes out on time, thereby preserving your boss's reputation, you then have the right to make a request when you want some special consideration. Build up these credits, and take advantage of them when the need arises.

Avoid unethical political practices. Also falling under the general heading of politics are some underhanded tactics that ultimately damage the careers of people who use them. Be sure not to use any of the following ploys:

1. *Discrediting a rival.* Speaking negatively about someone you're competing with for a position only makes you look bad.
2. *Covering up the truth.* Lying or omitting important information damages your credibility, often irreparably.
3. *Taking undue credit.* Making it appear that you did work or came up with ideas that really should be credited to someone else, such as your employees, generates resentment.
4. *Blackmail.* Don't threaten to reveal negative information about someone in power in order to pressure that person to do you a favor—you'll also generate a desire for revenge.

Defend yourself against devious politics. If someone treats you or others in the unethical ways we've mentioned, you will need to defend yourself. One way is to document the facts or your side of the story. If you have records that indicate what is really going on, you can use them to counter. You might also confront the person in private, indicating that you know what is going on and explaining why behaving ethically would be more advantageous in the long run. Your best defense, however, is to maintain a record of high integrity and good performance. Then, if people try to discredit you, they will not be believed.

CONCLUSION

From the outset of this book, we have maintained that the supervisory experience can be very demanding. It is your approach to those demands that will determine whether you earn the respect and cooperation of your bosses and employees — in short, whether or not you will succeed.

As we conclude, therefore, we challenge you to incorporate the techniques and guidelines we have presented here into your daily supervisory routine. Doing so will provide you with a solid foundation for approaching new situations and challenges creatively, thoughtfully — and successfully.

Good luck!

AVAILABLE FROM
SKILLPATH PUBLICATIONS

SELF-STUDY SOURCEBOOKS

Climbing the Corporate Ladder: What You Need to Know and Do to Be a Promotable Person *by Barbara Pachter and Marjorie Brody*

Coping With Supervisory Nightmares: 12 Common Nightmares of Leadership and What You Can Do About Them *by Michael and Deborah Singer Dobson*

Defeating Procrastination: 52 Fail-Safe Tips for Keeping Time on Your Side *by Marlene Caroselli, Ed.D.*

Discovering Your Purpose *by Ivy Haley*

Going for the Gold: Winning the Gold Medal for Financial Independence *by Lesley D. Bissett, CFP*

Having Something to Say When You Have to Say Something: The Art of Organizing Your Presentation *by Randy Horn*

Info-Flood: How to Swim in a Sea of Information Without Going Under *by Marlene Caroselli, Ed.D.*

The Innovative Secretary *by Marlene Caroselli, Ed.D.*

Letters & Memos: Just Like That! *by Dave Davies*

Mastering the Art of Communication: Your Keys to Developing a More Effective Personal Style *by Michelle Fairfield Poley*

Organized for Success! 95 Tips for Taking Control of Your Time, Your Space, and Your Life *by Nanci McGraw*

A Passion to Lead! How to Develop Your Natural Leadership Ability *by Michael Plumstead*

P.E.R.S.U.A.D.E.: Communication Strategies That Move People to Action *by Marlene Caroselli, Ed.D.*

Productivity Power: 250 Great Ideas for Being More Productive *by Jim Temme*

Promoting Yourself: 50 Ways to Increase Your Prestige, Power, and Paycheck *by Marlene Caroselli, Ed.D.*

Proof Positive: How to Find Errors Before They Embarrass You *by Karen L. Anderson*

Risk-Taking: 50 Ways to Turn Risks Into Rewards *by Marlene Caroselli, Ed.D. and David Harris*

Speak Up and Stand Out: How to Make Effective Presentations *by Nanci McGraw*

Stress Control: How You Can Find Relief From Life's Daily Stress *by Steve Bell*

The Technical Writer's Guide *by Robert McGraw*

Total Quality Customer Service: How to Make It Your Way of Life *by Jim Temme*

Write It Right! A Guide for Clear and Correct Writing *by Richard Andersen and Helene Hinis*

Your Total Communication Image *by Janet Signe Olson, Ph.D.*

HANDBOOKS

The ABC's of Empowered Teams: Building Blocks for Success *by Mark Towers*

Assert Yourself! Developing Power-Packed Communication Skills to Make Your Points Clearly, Confidently, and Persuasively *by Lisa Contini*

Breaking the Ice: How to Improve Your On-the-Spot Communication Skills *by Deborah Shouse*

The Care and Keeping of Customers: A Treasury of Facts, Tips, and Proven Techniques for Keeping Your Customers Coming BACK! *by Roy Lantz*

Challenging Change: Five Steps for Dealing With Change *by Holly DeForest and Mary Steinberg*

Dynamic Delegation: A Manager's Guide for Active Empowerment *by Mark Towers*

Every Woman's Guide to Career Success *by Denise M. Dudley*

Grammar? No Problem! *by Dave Davies*

Great Openings and Closings: 28 Ways to Launch and Land Your Presentations With Punch, Power, and Pizazz *by Mari Pat Varga*

Hiring and Firing: What Every Manager Needs to Know *by Marlene Caroselli, Ed.D. with Laura Wyeth, Ms.Ed.*

How to Be a More Effective Group Communicator: Finding Your Role and Boosting Your Confidence in Group Situations *by Deborah Shouse*

How to Deal With Difficult People *by Paul Friedman*

Learning to Laugh at Work: The Power of Humor in the Workplace *by Robert McGraw*

Making Your Mark: How to Develop a Personal Marketing Plan for Becoming More Visible and More Appreciated at Work *by Deborah Shouse*

Meetings That Work *by Marlene Caroselli, Ed.D.*

The Mentoring Advantage: How to Help Your Career Soar to New Heights *by Pam Grout*

Minding Your Business Manners: Etiquette Tips for Presenting Yourself Professionally in Every Business Situation *by Marjorie Brody and Barbara Pachter*

Misspeller's Guide *by Joel and Ruth Schroeder*

Motivation in the Workplace: How to Motivate Workers to Peak Performance and Productivity *by Barbara Fielder*

NameTags Plus: Games You Can Play When People Don't Know What to Say *by Deborah Shouse*

Networking: How to Creatively Tap Your People Resources *by Colleen Clarke*

New & Improved! 25 Ways to Be More Creative and More Effective *by Pam Grout*

Power Write! A Practical Guide to Words That Work *by Helene Hinis*

The Power of Positivity: Eighty ways to energize your life *by Joel and Ruth Schroeder*

Putting Anger to Work For You *by Ruth and Joel Schroeder*

Reinventing Your Self: 28 Strategies for Coping With Change *by Mark Towers*

Saying "No" to Negativity: How to Manage Negativity in Yourself, Your Boss, and Your Co-Workers *by Zoie Kaye*

The Supervisor's Guide: The Everyday Guide to Coordinating People and Tasks *by Jerry Brown and Denise Dudley, Ph.D.*

Taking Charge: A Personal Guide to Managing Projects and Priorities *by Michal E. Feder*

Treasure Hunt: 10 Stepping Stones to a New and More Confident You! *by Pam Grout*

A Winning Attitude: How to Develop Your Most Important Asset! *by Michelle Fairfield Poley*

For more information, call 1-800-873-7545.

NOTES

NOTES